CHRISTOPHE

ANNIVERSARY

ANNIVERSARY 4

THE LION OF LEMNOS 5

LUCIPHER 7

THE LANGUAGE OF LOVE 8

OUR DAUGHTER 9

LOBSTERS 10

AMAZONIAN 12

AUF DEM WASSER ZU SINGEN 13

ONE NIGHT ONLY 14

TWO COMMANDS 15

ANNIVERSARY

No more fervent celebrant than you
of birthdays, anniversaries and feasts
that broke the humdrum of the year, demanding
ceremony, gifts and merrymaking.

Our six privately sacred days
came round, came round and round again,
but, when your death fell a fortnight short of your birthday,
failed to complete the cycle, their twenty-ninth.
Instead, an anniversary was added
to my year, if not to yours.

Now the tenth approaches; and it will pass
without ceremony, without merriment.
But an exchange of gifts should still be possible:
poems from me to you, the memories
of which they are made
from you to me.

THE LION OF LEMNOS

Who pushed the tumbler?
I can't believe it was you,
neither of our guests
looked the likely culprit,
and it certainly wasn't me.
No, we were in earnest –
well-boozed but in earnest –
as the up-turned glass,
uncommonly roused and headstrong,
slid, paused, edged away,
hesitated and pounced
from letter to letter
in answer to our questions.

We had got through
to a certain Miss Lomax –
first name, dates of birth and death
undisclosed –
but speaking to us,
albeit with difficulty,
from somewhere in the middle
of the eighteenth century.
She wanted to tell us
about the Lion of Lemnos,
some old wrong, or shady business,
or misunderstanding
concerning it and the British Museum.
But what precisely?

She couldn't, or wouldn't, explain,
however hard we pressed her;
our pestering flustered her
and threw her into deeper
and more frequent silences;
we had lost her attention, her trust,
and she was withdrawing.
What put it into your head then
to ask her about next Saturday's
lottery numbers?
I remonstrated. Our friends laughed.
The game was over.
Diffident Miss Lomax
and her mysterious Lion
had fled, to remain – with you now –
unreachable on the far side.

LUCIPHER

The name we went by
when we shared an address
@compuserve.
You thought of it.

Straight away, I
adored its wit,
its mischief, its nerve,
its mongrelness.

In a word, we became –
for each other –
a marriage myth
of the cybersphere.

Then you died, and with
much administrative bother
and wear and tear
I forsook the name.

THE LANGUAGE OF LOVE

1

Mon poux,
contraction of *mon époux*:
endearment.
Louse for spouse!
From the topsy-turvy
language of love.
Mon p'tit poux:
the two *p*s making
a quickfire double kiss.
Thank you. Thank you.

2

Tu es une ange!
But *ange* is masculine
and you loved French too much
to let me get away
with such a solecism.
So I repeated it often,
as I do today
addressing you,
unmasculine angel!

OUR DAUGHTER

Our scary teenaged daughter
still hangs by a butcher's hook
through her topknot of ribbons
from the end of the bookcase.

Punk rag doll
of the zany, spacy, stitchwork eyes
and goth-black smirk,
she is used to being ignored.

Guests come and go –
otherwise talkative folk,
who haven't a word to say
either about her or to her.

Might it be the way she's dressed:
miniest of miniskirts,
lace-topped stockings, mismatched,
those trinkets and baubles?

Or her attitude, perhaps?
The taunt of her little, bare paunch?
Dumb insolence, hard to distinguish
from dumb appeal?

Dumbness must be catching!
No matter, social life
proceeds without her;
and she, ostentatiously, without it.

Effigy only child,
same age as when I gave her to you
as a wedding-anniversary present –
our twenty-first.

LOBSTERS

Kind Tom Lynch
gave us his cottage
in West Clare,
free of charge:
the ideal base
from which to launch
breezy forays
along that spectacular,
wind-assailed coast
and inland across
the austere, riven
karst plateau of the Burren.
Generous days!

And a generous evening
when Seamus and Marie
drove from Dublin
to dine with us.
'Brine-stung glut'
not far from my mind,
we obtained, not oysters,
but enormous lobsters
from the hatchery,
only to find
as they simmered in their pot
that our kitchen lacked
apparatus
to open them with.

No worries:
here was a hammer!
Passing it around,
we stooped to the stone floor
and whacked and whacked
at the samurai armour
with relish, with flair.
Feasting and mirth;
the laying down
of an unofficial memory;
what such times are for.

Isabel Godin des Odonais and you
met in a footnote
to Prescott's *History of the Conquest of Peru.*

It was identification at first sight,
and you started a play
such as nobody else would think to try to write.

It began with a song:
an Amazonian creation myth
made up by yourself and twenty-seven verses long.

Unfriendly Indians formed a Greek chorus
commenting on the party
of doomed European travellers you'd assembled for us.

Mme Godin was to be sole survivor,
but the expedition never got going.
Instead: pages and pages of typescript showing

all the research you'd done,
a jungle of data. How I wish you'd managed to put
her brave, three-thousand-mile journey on the stage;

and her husband there to welcome her
as she arrived,
distressed, in tatters and barefoot,

at the mouth of the Amazon.

AUF DEM WASSER ZU SINGEN

A certain landscape always got you going:
soft hills or downland, and the road ahead
amiably meandering out of sight.

At the wheel, some impulse of delight
would prompt a verse or two of Schubert's flowing,
6/8 melody. Now that you're dead,

Irmgard Seefried on CD must do instead,
though she can never hope to rival quite
your pitch of joy, windows wound down, breeze blowing.

Too few saw you in your last theatre rôle,
the affected hero of *La Forêt mouillée,*
Victor Hugo's seldom-performed verse play.
Cross-dressed, in white face, top hat and cutaway –
from my late father's wardrobe – you stole the show.

No, that's not it; that wasn't your style; you simply took
rightful possession of the part,
learnt pages of alexandrines off by heart,
flew to rehearsals in Provence and, fired
by months of Bernard's coaching and coaxing, acquired
the voice, gestures, gait and look that he desired,
and became, for one night only, *comédienne.*

Not *comédien.* Nobody in the hall
could have mistaken you for a man,
though, equally, nobody doubted you were French.
This being a Bernard production, the cast
included Indian dancers, opera singers, the village choir,
a vast ensemble, less theatre than carnival –
and starring you! You surpassed
even yourself. It was your most sublime performance
and your last.

TWO COMMANDS

Among the wise things you said
from your banked and raised hospice bed
were two commands to me.
One: that I should be
less inclined to procrastinate.
(Shameful to relate,
I promised I would – but not yet.)
The second, that I should get
married again
shocked and silenced me then;
yet I am happily married now,
as happily as I was,
and no doubt largely because
you showed me how
such happiness can be sought,
found, caught,
and kept by a shared will
through fortunes both good and ill,
or the mixture and muddle between.
You would know what I mean.

First published in 2015
by Enitharmon Press
10 Bury Place
London WC1A 2JL

www.enitharmon.co.uk

Distributed in the UK by
Central Books
99 Wallis Road
London E9 5LN

Distributed in the USA and Canada
by Independent Publishers Group
814 North Franklin Street
Chicago, IL 60610
USA
www.ipgbooks.com

ISBN: 978-1-910392-81-2

Enitharmon Press gratefully acknowledges
the financial support of Arts Council England,
through Grants for the Arts.

British Library Cataloguing-in-Publication Data.
A catalogue record for this book is available
from the British Library.

Typeset in 10pt Requiem
Designed by Rupert Gowar-Cliffe
Printed in Wales by Gomer Press